MW01492701

Helping the Homeless

A Service Guide

CHAPLAIN T. M. BABCOCK

A typical Saturday in Skid Row (Los Angeles 2014)

Photo by
Tina Babcock

Homelessness: An examination of the journey to recovery. Chaplain Babcock, having served for more than a decade in the heart of the Skid Row in Los Angeles, looks at some of the causes of homelessness and possible interventions. Just as in the Great Depression, we are seeing unprecedented natural disasters, unemployment, foreclosures, and a rise in substance abuse addictions. Homelessness is now a national epidemic. How does the average person, pastor, church, and government official make a difference in their community? This book gives practical advice for those asking this question.

WESTBOW
PRESS®
A DIVISION OF THOMAS NELSON
& ZONDERVAN

WestBow Press books may be ordered through booksellers or by contacting:

WestBow Press
A Division of Thomas Nelson & Zondervan
1663 Liberty Drive
Bloomington, IN 47403
www.westbowpress.com
1 (866) 928-1240

Because of the dynamic nature of the Internet, any web addresses or
links contained in this book may have changed since publication and
may no longer be valid. The views expressed in this work are solely those
of the author and do not necessarily reflect the views of the publisher,
and the publisher hereby disclaims any responsibility for them.

Any people depicted in stock imagery provided by Thinkstock are
models, and such images are being used for illustrative purposes only.
Certain stock imagery © Thinkstock.

Scripture quotes marked (KJV) are taken from
the King James Version of the Bible.

Scripture quotations taken from the New American Standard Bible® (NASB),
Copyright © 1960, 1962, 1963, 1968, 1971, 1972, 1973, 1975, 1977, 1995
by The Lockman Foundation. Used by permission. www.Lockman.org

Scripture quotations marked TLB are taken from The Living Bible
copyright 1971. Used by permission of Tyndale House Publishers,
Inc., Carol Stream, Illinois 60188. All rights reserved.

ISBN: 978-1-5127-8014-7 (sc)
ISBN: 978-1-5127-8016-1 (hc)
ISBN: 978-1-5127-8015-4 (e)

Library of Congress Control Number: 2017903980

Print information available on the last page.

WestBow Press rev. date: 4/13/2017

Foreword

We live in a society where what was once called "normal" in America has ceased to exist. Our definition of family, marriage, and even Christianity is at risk of being squeezed into a little bucket that we call *"politically correct."* Unfortunately, the tear in the safety net for our social programs, charitable choices, and benevolence collections is getting wider, and our well-meaning efforts do not even come close to addressing the very real problem in our country called *homelessness.*

Chaplain Tina Babcock, affectionately called *Pastor Tina*, has penned this great work, *Homelessness: A Worker's Guide*, to assist those who have been called to help the multitudes who have slipped into this new lifestyle category and to serve our brothers and sisters more efficiently. This work also displays a practical guide for learning from a tried and proven ground-level leader from the heart of Skid Row in Los Angeles, California. From a Christian worldview, supported by her education in psychology, this guide will help provide the wisdom and the heart needed to "cause no further damage" when working with this expanding and vulnerable population.

The apostle Paul warned the newly formed church in Rome that a good heart and good intentions are not enough. "For I bear them record that they have a zeal of God, but not according to knowledge" (Rom. 10:2). We need a practical guide from a seasoned worker to minimize the pitfalls that will come … and maximize the results that will store up treasures in heaven for us and help our neighbors in their journey *back home*, while we are here on earth.

If your calling to ministry includes reaching out to the homeless population, I strongly suggest that you prayerfully read this material. This book will help give you a real look at this growing problem while providing you with tools to make a positive difference in the lives of many.

Rev. Dr. Wade A. Kyle

Contents

CHAPTER 1

An Introduction to Homelessness: The Rising Tide in America

Thank you for your interest and concern for helping those who are homeless in the United States. We are the solution, one person at a time, making a difference in one person's or one family's lives. I have been working with this population for about two decades and know the immense joy of helping just one individual come out from a place of despair and social isolation.

Let me tell you of just one of the many individuals I met in my travels through the United States, working with rescue missions in the urban centers of several cities. My initial impression of Sheba (a pseudonym to protect her real identity) was that she had been on the streets a long time. She had the look of someone most of us would cross the street to avoid. But when I looked past the grunge and the tattered clothes and really looked at her, I realized she was beautiful. Her hair was cropped close to her head, and her clothes were dirty, the kind of dirt that has been there long enough to become part of the fabric. When she spoke, you could see she had no teeth. She probably had them all pulled due to the destruction from drug use and neglect. But even with all of that, it was clear she had once been an incredibly beautiful woman. She was *still* beautiful. The cropped hair revealed stunning dark-brown eyes, high cheekbones, and perfect features reminiscent of Ethiopian royalty. Her long neck and graceful, long arms and legs made it impossible for her to be less than poetry in motion.

As she spoke, her language seemed at first unintelligible. Then slowly I began to realize she was making sense, but her speech was so rapid it was difficult to distinguish one word from another. As her story unfolded, I learned that she had been on the streets of the inner city for more than a decade. Everyone on the streets thought she was crazy, and that worked to her advantage. She would stand in the middle of the street and talk loudly to what observers thought were her hallucinations. She explained that she was really talking to herself out loud. She would have full conversations with herself, and it made people think she was crazy. That made her less desirable and therefore, safer from those who prey on our most vulnerable citizens. You'd never know what this loud, crazy woman might do!

She had been doing this for years, and her speech had gotten faster and faster because she knew what she was saying; there was no need to slow down or articulate each word properly. Staying dirty was also safer than cleaning up and smelling good. Rapes of women on the street were a daily occurrence in her world. The urban centers of our nation are dangerous places for any woman alone, but especially the marginalized homeless woman. One woman was kicked to death as she slept on the sidewalk. Another woman was set on fire while she slept in a car. Though badly burned, she survived.

Sheba had finally gotten sick and tired of the life on the street; she was ready for a change. Up until now, she couldn't imagine her life getting any better. She had had an encounter with God that had evoked new hope. One of her old friends from the streets had come into a Christian rescue mission and experienced real transformation. Her friend had shown her the possibility that her life could be different too.

The mission staff spent weeks teaching her to slow down her speech so she could be understood. She got new dentures and new clothes and began to find herself again in the safety and love of the mission family. She was so transformed that she had to identify herself to her old connections. They hugged her and were amazed at the change.

She taught me a lot about how far down a person can go and still rise again to find his or her dignity. This is a book about the people we as a society minimize and throw away. These are precious people who hide in the shadows of our cities.

Why write a book about homelessness? The typical American of the twentieth century only heard about homelessness occurring in other countries. Technically there were some people who didn't live in homes in the United States, and we referred to them as bums, hobos, and "no accounts." In the twenty-first century, we are no longer shocked by the homeless person pushing the shopping cart, carrying all his or her worldly possessions down the street. Not since the Great Depression, when there were large numbers of unemployed and displaced persons, have we had the level of homelessness we are seeing in America. I have worked with homeless individuals for many years. I have worked in the heart of Skid Row with people on the streets, with people in homeless shelters, and with people who are homeless because of drug and/or alcohol addictions. In 2014, the Department of Housing and Urban Development (HUD) counted 113,952 homeless individuals just in California. The numbers of children living on the streets or in shelters has been steadily rising. There are more than half a million homeless in the United States (Meghan Henry 8). This calamity affects us all.

My personal brush with homelessness was brief—just a few months. If you had asked me, I probably wouldn't have identified myself as "homeless." At eleven years old, I had no idea what it must have been like for my parents to be responsible for two children—with no money, no jobs, and no home. I'll share more about this later. My personal introduction to homelessness was short-lived because good friends of my parents took us all in and let us stay with them until my parents could secure jobs and a place to live.

I have had a couple of personal acquaintances who found themselves temporarily displaced so they stayed in my home over the years. One of these guests was only supposed to be with us for a week or so while she made other arrangements. That week turned into a year, and when I pressed her about her options, I will never forget the emphatic way in which she informed me that she was "not homeless." She was just going through a difficult patch. She was sure that I was implying that she was a negligent and untrustworthy person. She said the word *homeless* as though it implied the lowest level of humanity. She had always been able to be gainfully employed until a crisis left her unable to work and eventually homeless. It was difficult to discuss the obstacles to her finding housing because the stigma of homelessness made the topic so toxic. She was a successful career person and raised her children in an affluent environment. Now she didn't have a reasonable income, and it made getting accepted for rentals in a competitive rental market almost impossible.

She certainly is not alone in this. I have known many others who have had similar challenges. Single parents are often severely challenged in finding affordable housing and having enough in savings to help them maintain their housing through a layoff.

The Foster Care System Is Contributing to Homelessness

This woman, like many who find themselves without housing options, didn't have a network of support at the time she needed it most. When I was eighteen, I had a friend help me understand the implications of not having a network of support. I was living out on my own, and as a struggling community college student, most of my meals consisted of rice and a donated chocolate milk drink from a charity. However, in a pinch, I knew my mom or my brothers would help me out if I could swallow my pride enough to ask. She, on the other hand, was orphaned at a young age when her parents were killed in an accident. She was raised in the foster care system, and when she was eighteen, she was sent out on her own. She managed to get a scholarship to go to college, but she didn't have anyone in her life who was there for her if anything happened. There was no family to rejoin during school holidays and breaks. No one was there to give her advice or help if she couldn't pay her electric bill.

Every year, there are thousands of kids who "age out" of the foster care system and have a similar story. Depending on their placements, they may be totally unprepared for life on their own. They often have severe emotional trauma in their past that interferes with their ability to build healthy relationships. They may never have experienced a truly healthy relationship in their lives. All they have known is chaos.

According to a 2014 HUD study, 194,000 children and youth were homeless with their family in January 2014 in the United States. An additional 45,205 children and youth (all under eighteen) were homeless on their own without an adult (Meghan Henry 3). The majority of the prison population in America has been through the foster care system—in some states as high as 90 percent (Thoma). There is no way to know how much of that correlation is cause and effect, but it is certainly something to consider. Many of these individuals left their foster care placements when they became teenagers.

There have been some studies showing a decrease in

homeless numbers in the past decade, with more attention given to this travesty. However, I predict that we will continue to see the numbers of homeless individuals grow. I believe that some of the decreases are a result of more hidden homeless individuals as cities try to push out those homeless encampments that make their numbers look bad. City officials often move the problem around rather than solve it. I believe all of us are going to be faced with some family member or friend knocking on our door with no place to go. Has it happened to you yet? If not, just wait for another deeper recession, and it will impact you or someone you know.

A Little History

Allow me to take a moment to give you a little background on how I came to be considered by some as an "expert" on homelessness. I had no idea how my personal history was preparing me for a career working with this vulnerable population. I was raised in a fairly average military family, with two parents and two brothers. Though the military kept us moving from state to state, living in a variety of settings, the navy was our home. I grew up feeling that wherever they sent us was just where we laid our head for the moment. That developed both a strong sense of family, the only constant, and a sense of adventure. I learned that people are pretty much the same wherever you go, just wrapped in different customs.

As a child of eleven years old, my family was homeless for just a few months after my father retired from the military. Dad had been in the navy for twenty years, and his deployments had left little opportunity to see his parents in Illinois, or my mother's family in Texas. My parents decided to take a cross-country trip before settling into new jobs in California. The trip went well, going by car through Texas, then north to Illinois and back again. Well almost … when we reached Arizona on the return trip, the engine in our old Buick began smoking like a house on fire. The engine had overheated, the engine block had cracked, and there was no repairing it. That left us stranded until a new engine could be shipped to the local mechanic and put in place. The cost of the new engine wiped out almost everything my parents had saved to resettle in California. The four of us—Mom, Dad, one older brother, age seventeen, and me—camped in a national park for a couple weeks. I remember one day when it rained so hard we took shelter in the tent for the day; my father turned to Mom and said, "Well, honey, I promised I'd always keep a roof over your head!" That was the moment I knew this was not just a camping trip. We actually didn't have a home.

We weren't worried about that before the trip, because we had money to get a hotel until we found a rental, but now we had to use most of that money on fixing the car. We didn't know exactly what the future held. Mom and I spent time looking at home magazines (our version of HGTV) dreaming about the perfect house. Once the car was fixed and we returned to California, we were taken into the home of friends until Mom and Dad could begin working and save enough to pay first and last month's rent. There are many families that are experiencing similar circumstances in this time of financial recession. Some are not as fortunate as we were, to have good friends with both the capacity and willingness to come to our rescue.

The New Homeless: Couch Surfing and the Drive-through Life

There is a form of homelessness referred to as "coach surfing." This is when someone, usually a single adult, doesn't have any place to go, and he or she just goes to one friend's house, stays a few days or a week or so, and then moves to another friend's house, and repeat, repeat, repeat! They sleep on their friends' or acquaintances' couches, trying not to wear out their welcome at each place. Some families are living in a good Samaritan's garage because they can't find housing. There are many families living in their cars. Anyone who has experienced an eviction even if it wasn't his or her fault, will find it almost impossible to be accepted as a renter. It may have been because of an ugly divorce, a foreclosure, or a family member's bad behavior, but the impact will follow anyone whose name was on the lease or rental application. With the advent of computer technology and Internet access to people's rental history, information previously unavailable to landlords can now be traced back decades and bar them from housing almost indefinitely. Now landlords routinely look at credit history and any arrests as reasons to deny housing.

Sometimes all it takes to create homelessness is a shortage of rental units. In June of 2016 a study showed that Los Angeles needed an additional 382,000 rental units to keep up with demand. So where do those individuals represented in that statistic go? In a market like this, landlords can pick from the cream of the crop of applicants, and anyone who has a low credit rating, no credit rating, a mental illness, a record of incarceration, or just too many kids will be pushed to the curb. Even shelters generally won't take anyone with more than three children. Parents become afraid to ask for help for fear their children will be taken by social services for not providing adequately for their children.

Domestic Violence and Homelessness

My first exposure working with homeless individuals and families came when I began working at Battered Women's Services in San Diego. The YWCA, the parent organization, has a long history of intervening in the lives of women in need. As a counselor in their shelter, I helped many women and families deal with the crisis of suddenly having to leave a home that was no longer safe. Though the traumas of violence they had suffered were severe, it was sometimes the trauma of being homeless that had a greater impact on their lives. It was often the need to recover their home that drove many of them back into unsafe relationships. I had many conversations with women who just couldn't walk away from their house and belongings. They had to leave their home and hide, because they couldn't remain safely in their own home. Even if their partner was arrested, they were usually released in a short time. Court-ordered restraining orders can help show a history of abuse and help in prosecution of a batterer, but they don't protect a person if the batterer chooses to ignore the order. Temporary restraining orders only work as a protective device with rational, law-abiding individuals; to a batterer it is just a piece of paper.

I remember one woman who said she had inherited many family treasures, including antique furniture that had been passed down for many generations. She just couldn't walk away and see it all destroyed. She shared how she had risked her life to stay long enough to try to remove her treasures before leaving. Many individuals move their things into a storage unit until they can find housing. But many lose everything if they can't keep up the storage fees. Think about the loss of all your worldly possessions when you see a homeless woman pushing a shopping cart loaded to overflowing with personal items. How heartbreaking it is to see someone who has ended up in a place where the total of his or her life's material possessions now fit in a shopping cart. Some of the women in shelters will hoard things like bottles of shampoo or other hygiene products. It is as though they needed to have a sense of owning something, anything!

Homelessness in Skid Row

In 1997 I was recruited to work for the Los Angeles Mission's Anne Douglas Center in heart of Los Angeles's Skid Row. They have a Christian recovery program specifically designed for those with drug and/or alcohol addictions that have resulted in homelessness or incarceration. This area of the city is really called Central City, but the term *Skid Row* has become slang for any depressed urban area known for its cheap hotels, homelessness, and prostitution. The term's derivation is disputed, but some believe it was originally coined in Seattle Washington because an area called Skid Road, where logs were dragged to the mill. It was an area that was lined with brothels, cheap hotels, and liquor establishments. A person who couldn't earn a living wage was said to be destined to go down Skid Road. I had formerly worked in San Diego's version of Skid Row in a domestic violence shelter. The domestic violence shelter was definitely a cleaner, more hospitable place to work than the homeless shelter of that city in 1990. I was very hesitant to see what a rescue mission in Los Angeles's Skid Row would look like, but I was pleasantly surprised. The Los Angeles Mission's facility was clean and well maintained. Their women's facility, the Anne Douglas Center was beautiful. Most our clients were from very impoverished roots, but not all. Some had just been derailed by some cataclysmic life circumstance. I also had the opportunity to travel throughout the United States and work with directors of programs in many cities. I had an opportunity to see homelessness in both small and large cities, rural and urban. The Los Angeles Mission (LAM) was a forerunner in providing wraparound services to those who are homeless and those who were addicted to alcohol and other drugs. I had the opportunity to meet with homeless service workers from other countries who came to LAM to learn about working with those with substance abuse issues.

The program was a year in length, and the graduates of the program had an option to stay in one of their transitional housing units for an additional six months to a year. During their first year, the mission required them to be involved in counseling, support groups, spiritual development, work assignments, social events, and academic studies. All of this was offered within the safety of their temporary residency in the mission. It was as much an education for me as it was for our residents. I worked first as a lead chaplain and later an executive director. I worked with other chaplains, acting as counselors and case managers. We learned that the obstacles to sobriety and social stability are more complicated than one would think. Sometimes homelessness itself was the reason they started using drugs. We learned that what led to homelessness, drug use, and instability of many kinds often began when they didn't fit into the structure of the American educational system. Perhaps it was because there was no stability at home; sometimes it was because they had an undiagnosed learning disability and were told they were just too stupid to learn. Lack of stability and proper modeling at home impeded their success not only in school but also in the workplace. Keeping a job and being promoted to higher-wage positions requires appropriate social skills.

Many of the adults we worked with had never had the social skills and work ethics required to maintain traditional employment modeled for them. Some of them came from families that were multigenerational addicts and/or criminals. Some of their families had been living on welfare for generations and had never been challenged to learn the skills necessary to become self reliant. They seldom had both parents in their lives, and whoever raised them (they were often bounced from one foster care placement to another or from one relative to another) didn't prepare them for a nine-to-five life of employment.

Once a person is an adult, very little social mentoring takes place. If a person is inappropriate, most people just reject them. As chaplains, we often had to assist them in basic social interactions. I remember a woman who, whenever she had a conflict with someone, would lean in and put her face right in the other person's face and make challenging remarks. She was so intimidating that no one wanted to work with her. I have no doubt she learned this behavior in her family, and it was probably very effective with the bullies she had to deal with. One day I mimicked her behavior and then told her that this body language was a big part of why people didn't want to work with her. She was shocked and offended. She emphatically told me she didn't do that. We had to agree to disagree, until a day later she came back, clearly astonished that she had caught herself doing the very thing I had demonstrated. If she hadn't been in counseling, I doubt she would ever have learned how she was contributing to being socially ostracized.

A Life of Crime and Incarceration with No Way Out

Though someone who has poor social skills or is already financially on the edge is more vulnerable to become homeless, I have met people from all walks of life who have found themselves drug addicted or just destitute and lacking the resources to live independently. Some people are homeless because of their own bad behavior. They may have acted out because of poor examples at home, a substance abuse issue, a life crisis, or mental illness. Some may have participated in criminal activity. Some individuals choose crime as a shortcut to success. However a criminal lifestyle isn't always a choice. I worked with many who came from families that were deeply imbedded in gang life styles. Their families had been part of the gang for many generations. It really wasn't a choice to join or not join. For these individuals, sobriety and leaving the criminal lifestyle often meant having to give up relationships with their families, childhood friends, and neighbors. One woman, who was born to parents who had very low IQs, was registered with Social Services as also being impaired mentally. Her parents did this primarily so she could get a regular Social Security check. Her parents received this check from the time she was a child into her adult life. In addition to living off her social security check, they taught her the family business, which was selling illegal drugs. She really wasn't deficient mentally and was highly successful selling drugs. She became addicted herself and eventually sought help from the mission. We helped her realize that she had a good brain and could be successful in a normal non-criminal lifestyle. Her parents had been supportive of her getting free help and getting off of drugs. However, her decision to leave behind the criminal lifestyle and stop supporting her parents was not received well. It was heartbreaking to see this woman have to fight with her own parents to stay in a life of sobriety and freedom. I admire the many men and women I have known who have left those roots behind and against great odds have begun new lives. I am also impressed with those who were strong enough to resist the temptations of that lifestyle and later reached out to family and friends to point the way to a happier life.

Overmedicating Our Veterans Has Produced Homelessness

There are many veterans among the homeless. Many of our veterans returned from tours of duty that left them injured and in need of pain medication. Many of these prescribed pain medications have serious addiction potential and have been handed out like candy by uninformed doctors. Some pharmaceutical companies even told doctors these medications were not addictive when given for legitimate pain. Many of our veterans developed addictions that were not properly treated, and they have become homeless as a result of their addiction. Some of our veterans have returned from the theatre of war with brain injuries and psychological damage. The Veterans Administration has been ill equipped to deal with the large numbers of veterans needing specialized treatment, and many veterans have gone untreated and ended up homeless (Kuhnhenn).

Homelessness and the Mentally Ill

There are large numbers of individuals who are homeless and have a mental disorder. If a person has a substance abuse disorder and a mental illness, he or she is considered to have "co-occurring disorders" or to be "dual diagnosed." For a long time, services weren't available for dual-diagnosed individuals. The numbers of individuals who fit this category grew, and service providers started advocating for funding to assist them. Now co-occurring disorders is so common almost all homeless and addiction treatment service organizations accept them for treatment. I believe the numbers are so large because we have tied society's hands, preventing help to the mentally ill by inappropriate legislation. We have legislated their rights in such a way that their freedom of choice outweighs their need for treatment. I would like to suggest that when a person's perceptions of reality are severely impaired, there is no freedom to choose. We need to change the laws to include a provision for involuntary placement in a safe environment, until they can provide that for themselves. If we can do this for minors, we should be able to create appropriate legislation for those who suffer similar judgment impairment. This will require the availability of appropriate treatment resources. This lack of quality treatment resources is probably a big factor in the resistance to changing the laws.

According to HUD's 2013 Annual Homelessness Assessment Report, of those who experience homelessness, approximately 257,300 people have a severe mental illness or a chronic substance use disorder. Legislation passed in 1963, the Community Mental Health Centers

Act, made it unlawful to detain mentally ill people against their will if they were not currently a danger to themselves or others (Kofman). The practical application of the law has resulted in ignoring any dangers that are not imminent physical violence against oneself or another. Once people have reached the addiction phase of substance abuse, they, like other mental disorders, are not fully in control of their actions. Prior to 1963, due to the inappropriate institutionalization of individuals who were not mentally ill, the laws swung to an extreme. Now mentally ill people can be so delusional as to not know who they are and not be able to maintain a safe living environment, but they cannot be forced to get treatment.

I have worked with mentally ill senior adults who have been so impacted by dementia that they could not find their way back to their home, even if they went just a few blocks to the market. They might not remember their own name, but police would not detain them, and doctors would not send them for inpatient treatment. If no family member reported them as missing and they did not become violent or suicidal, they would be left to wander aimlessly with no help. I worked for a few years as an adult protective social worker. I would sometimes be called to aid people like this, if they appeared to be in distress or causing a problem for a community member or business. If I could find out who they were and who, if anyone, was caring for them, I could help; but if they were resistant to help, there was little I could legally do. The only thing that could be done was to convince a police officer or physician to request that they be held under Section 5150 of the California Welfare and Institutions Code, which authorizes them to involuntarily confine a person suspected to be severely mentally unstable. This was often difficult if not impossible to do. Police officers are not mental health professionals, and they often are reluctant to make an evaluation that goes beyond identifying if a crime has been committed or not. If I could get them to take the person to a psychiatric facility, the next hurdle was with the facility staff. The psychiatric facility personnel would then confine the person up to seventy-two hours to make further evaluations on the person's state of mind. A second hold of fourteen days may be added if it seemed warranted. In my experience, having been a government social worker and as a Skid Row chaplain, they are seldom held for more than the seventy-two hours regardless of their inability to provide for themselves long term. Most were turned out within twenty-four hours.

The second factor in the release of individuals who have debilitating mental health issues is that of money. The individuals who do not want treatment are not going to pay for a private care facility (even if they have the money), and public facilities are few and overburdened. Government-funded facilities seem to be motivated to release patients as quickly as possible, regardless of their mental state (Kofman). If there is no one to advocate for the patients, they are often put out at the first opportunity. This frequently is the only option for the underfunded and overcrowded service provider who copes with the disparity between available resources versus the volume of needs.

Civil rights organizations often fight any attempt to change the laws. They contend that citizens have the right to personal freedom and self-determination, even if they have debilitating mental illnesses. They would also contend that the government and family members have abused the ability to confine people in the past. They are correct on both counts. Prior to the 1963 legislation, family members were able to use the unproven claim that someone is mentally ill as a way of robbing him or her of personal property and parental rights. However, these rights could still be protected by additional safeguards in the process and written into the statutes, without leaving thousands to live in shelters and on the streets when they are truly not capable of evaluating their own sanity.

I believe we can protect the dignity and rights of the mentally ill more appropriately if we include in those rights the right to treatment, even when they are incapable of realizing their need for it. We do not ask our children if they want to go to school or stay in a safe environment. They are required to go wherever society deems meets the standards of a safe environment. We do this for children because they cannot understand the long-term consequences of living in the streets or of not having an education. In the same way, a person who is mentally impaired may not be able to see the long-term cost of refusing treatment.

Most mentally ill are not violent and are not a threat to others. However the number of individuals who are acting out with violence seems to be increasing. I believe that in many cases their rights to physical freedom, to come and go as they please, have prevented their getting treatment, which could have eliminated such tragedies. The increase in the use of synthetic drugs is also causing a rise in those who become violent when drug impaired. Even marijuana, which traditionally didn't cause violent behavior, in its synthetic forms can cause aggressive behavior for some users.

We don't need to swing back to the days when practically anyone could put a family member away to rot in an institution, but our system is broken and we need to fix it. Listen to the political dialogue around the recent mass murders and you will notice that the individual often displayed serious impairment in judgment, often threatening harm to others. When it was determined that there was no legal basis for detaining him or her as a criminal, there was almost never any attempt to do so on the basis of his or her mental state. Ask yourself, "Is a person who is seriously threatening homicide mentally stable?" Prior to the increase in terrorist incidents in the United States, common practice by most law enforcement was that if person making general threats hadn't named an individual, there were no grounds for either incarceration or as someone in need of in-patient treatment. So if I say "I am going to kill somebody," no action. If I say, "I am going to kill Jane Doe," I can be detained. The tragedies of the lost lives both of the perpetrators and victims are continually blamed on the weapons used and not on a broken mental health system and the lack of laws to facilitate mental health assistance.

Labels that Perpetuate Homelessness

No matter the cause, once a person falls into that hole of homelessness, it is very difficult to climb out. Once a label is placed on a person, like: "criminal," "addict," or "homeless," society naturally treats them with suspicion and isolates them. So what happens when a person turns over a new leaf, chooses the high road, and learns his or her lesson? Well, not much is different in societal responses. This tends to keep people locked into criminal and/or impoverished life circumstances. This is often the driving force in the life of someone who is chronically homeless or one who appears to choose homelessness as a lifestyle. These are the people who have tired of banging their heads against a brick wall. They are tired of the rejection and failures. I predict that we will continue to see the numbers of individuals who fall into this category of long-term homelessness grow.

Has It Happened to You Yet?

Sooner or later, I imagine we are all going to be faced with some family member or friend knocking on our door with no place to go. Has it happened to you yet? If not, just wait for another deeper recession and it will impact you or someone you know. Not everyone who reads this book is going to become a homelessness service worker, but I would challenge you that everyone is going to be faced with the question of, "What do I do when I see an individual or family in need?"

I hope that you will find the answers you need as you explore this topic. Please share this resource with those you know that can make a difference in our community. Share with those in your sphere of influence.

Share with local media and with government officials. Most importantly, become more informed about how you can personally help those who face one of the most devastating of life circumstances, the loss of being able to call a place home!

CHAPTER 2

Why Are Most Homeless Assistance Programs Faith Based?

Why do so many homeless resources emphasize the spiritual? The frequent pairing of spiritual help with practical resources for the homeless is as much about those who help as it is about the needs of the person who is homeless. Homelessness can't help but impact a person spiritually because it impacts every area of a life. It can impact people's identity, challenge their religious beliefs, and bring depression and despair. However, people who are homeless can also be quite spiritually mature and not in need of any real tutelage on spiritual issues. They may simply need housing and the kindness of a non-judgmental friend. Jesus of Nazareth, known by some as a remarkable rabbi, prophet, and teacher and by others as the Son of God, said: "Foxes have holes and birds have nests, but the Son of Man [referring to himself] has no place to lay his head" (New American Standard Bible, Matthew 8.20). There is a long history of holy men who have left all worldly possessions to seek a higher level of spiritual awareness, to leave behind the love of material wealth, and to seek a higher purpose. This is not the kind of homelessness we are seeking to help. There is a vast difference between the person who has his or her home taken from him or her, whether by the forces of nature or man, and the person who willingly walks away from the traditional life in a house. Most chronically homeless individuals have chosen to embrace, rather than fight their economic circumstances. They leave behind self-pity and the definitions of helplessness by adapting to a homeless lifestyle. This choice sometimes can be a misguided defensive response to hopelessness. They have come to believe there is no hope to get out of their impoverished, jobless, homeless state and have decided to embrace it rather than continue to seek solutions. For the person who has lost hope, that hope has to be rekindled through practical help before any long-term solution can be found. They need help in redefining themselves as part of a society that has rejected them.

So ask yourself, who would you go to if you needed hope? The local welfare office? A house of faith? Almost every charitable organization in America has its roots in people of faith. Most of the first pilgrims came fleeing religious persecution. Many came because of poverty and a class system devoid of hope. The first universities, hospitals, and sanitariums where created by people of faith. The Bible is full of admonitions to provide practical help to those in need. The brother of Jesus, James, wrote in the epistle named after him, in the second chapter, verses 15–16: "If you have a friend who is in need of food and clothing, and you say to him, "Well, good-bye and God bless you; stay warm and eat hearty," and then don't give him clothes or food, what good does that do?" (NASB).

The doctrines of the faith closely tied to Abraham are uniquely suited to producing a willingness in the follower to reach out to those who are homeless. Charity is a long-standing tradition of Islamic, Jewish, and Christian traditions. Giving is not based on the worthiness of the recipient, but on the character of the giver. Each of these faiths teaches that the poor are also created by God and as His creations He loves them as His children. If you want to have the favor of a parent, you had better treat their children well! Here are just a few admonitions from the Old and New Testaments of the Bible:

> When you help the poor you are lending to the Lord—and he pays wonderful interest on your loan! (Proverbs 19:17 TLB, paraphrased)

Give, and it will be given to you. They will pour into your lap a good measure—pressed down, shaken together, and running over. For by your standard of measure it will be measured to you in return (NASB, Luke 6.38).

If there is a poor man with you, one of your brothers, in any of your towns in your land which the Lord your God is giving you, you shall not harden your heart, nor close your hand from your poor brother (NASB, Deut. 15.7).

Pure and undefiled religion in the sight of our God and Father is this: to visit orphans and widows in their distress, and to keep oneself unstained by the world (NASB. James 1.27).

Give to everyone who asks of you, and whoever takes away what is yours, do not demand it back. Treat others the same way you want them to treat you (NASB, Luke 6.30.31).

You shall not charge interest to your
countrymen: interest on money, food, or
anything that may be loaned at interest
(NASB, Deut. 23.19).

For I was hungry, and you gave Me something to eat; I was thirsty, and you gave Me
something to drink; I was a stranger, and
you invited Me in (NASB, Matt. 25.35)

For though we have never yet seen God,
when we love each other God lives in us,
and his love within us grows ever stronger.
(1 John 4:12 TLB, paraphrased)

So who are these spiritual givers? It isn't just those
who claim allegiance to organized religions who give to
the poor. The famous psychologist Erik Erikson taught
that part of the development of a mature person was
to be able to see beyond his or her own desires and see
the needs of others. A mature person gives back to the
next generation, to the community, and to those less
fortunate than him or herself. There are those that have
caught the vision that life is better when we give of
ourselves to others. Unselfish giving is transformative.
Some people first encounter God and as a result of that

relationship, they feel loved and have a desire to love others. Some people discover God as they start reaching out to others and showing love. God inhabits love. Some of Jesus's disciples came to him one day to tell him that there was an "unauthorized" disciple doing miracles, recorded in the gospel of Mark.

John said to Him, "Teacher, we saw someone casting out demons in Your name, and we tried to prevent him because he was not following us." But Jesus said, "Do not hinder him, for there is no one who will perform a miracle in My name, and be able soon afterward to speak evil of Me. For he who is not against us is for us (NASB, Mark 9.38-40)

I have seen many volunteers working with the homeless who have come to a faith in God just by observing how God intervenes in the lives of those who sometimes seem beyond help.

CHAPTER 3

Who's that Sleeping on My Couch?

Taking a homeless person into your home is seldom a good idea. Now before you begin to attack me as a horrible person—hear me out. I didn't say it might not be a "God idea," just not a good idea. My husband and I have had a number of people stay with us over our more than forty years of married life. Some were family, some were friends, and only a couple of times were they a recent acquaintance. Once, in my morning devotions I read 1 Timothy 3 about the necessity of a leader in the church to be "given to hospitality." The Living Bible says he must like having people in his home. That same day I came in contact with someone who needed a place to stay. Normally I would be the first one to talk with her about resources and give her referrals to professionals who help those who are homeless. But before I could open my mouth, I heard very clearly in my mind and spirit, *An elder shall be given to hospitality.* I knew without a doubt God was telling me to ask the woman to stay with us. I knew I needed to obey but I wasn't excited about doing so, especially with someone I had just met. I decided in that moment to take the risk and I told her that it would just be temporary. She could have a few days to figure out what she was going to do, and my husband would have to agree first.

That began a year of shared residency. I really didn't know what I was signing up for when I gave that initial invitation. I am going to try to share my very human response to sharing my residence with a stranger. I hope that through sharing this experience, it will help you understand some of the challenges in helping those who can't find housing. You may be reading this because you have someone in your home now. Or you may be getting ready to open a house for the homeless. If you are a service worker, you might think you would never take someone into your home that was not appropriate, "This would never happen to me!" I highly recommend if you work with homeless individuals on a daily basis, that you try and keep your home as a sanctuary where you can decompress. It is spiritually and emotionally taxing work, and most of us need some time to rejuvenate. That being said, the truth is it will probably happen to all of us eventually. There are just so many people in need. You may bring relatives into your home thinking you know them and are so surprised by things you would never have thought would be an issue. It is just plain difficult to live with another human being! Most newlyweds are shocked that their sweetheart is never quite as perfect as they supposed—they get crumbs in the bed, leave the lights on, or leave their clothing lying all over the floor. You know the stuff that in the grand scheme of things isn't all that important, but in day-to-day living, it can be quite annoying.

As I said, this wasn't the first time Paul (my husband) and I had a live-in guest. We had a colleague live with us for three years. Our eldest daughter and her husband lived with us for a year while they both finished college before setting up their own household. We cared for my mother in our home the last eighteen months of her life. We have had some good friends stay with us for several months, so we weren't strangers to sharing a residence. Two things made this very different. One was that the woman was not our family or even a friend, and we had an expectation that this was a temporary arrangement. There was also a lack of trust because we hadn't had any time to get to know her under other circumstances. That lack of familiarity made it much harder to have her in our home. It was the fear of the unknown.

So here is what we learned that I felt deserved a

chapter—things are never what they seem! There is a romantic notion that many people have about helping the homeless. People who are homeless come from all backgrounds, all ethnicities, and all social classes. Are there more homeless people from poor or even criminal backgrounds? Yes! The reason there are more people from poor backgrounds is that they have less of a safety net—no big savings account or diversified investments to cash in when times get hard. However, I have worked with stockbrokers, successful artists, preachers, and teachers who have found themselves without resources and in need of help. I have worked with a lot of people who have become homeless as a result of alcohol, drug, or gambling addictions. But there are a lot of addicts of every kind who have jobs and homes. What people who are homeless have in common is that for some reason, they have lost access to resources. The reason for that loss is sometimes obvious, like a hurricane destroyed their home and their community. But sometimes it is because they don't know how to live with people. I have met many people who, in an attempt to deal with their own history of unfairly stereotyping homeless individuals as being a bad people, have gone to the other extreme and decided all homeless individuals are just nice people who have fallen on hard times. The truth is they are just people. They run the gambit from sinner to saint, clean to dirty, safe to very unsafe, and all the shades of gray in between! They pretty much mirror the rest of society. Anyone can be the victim of financial catastrophe.

It is true that not being nice or not knowing how to get along with people can make it much harder to bounce back from the loss of financial resources. Not knowing how to get along with others can lead to divorce, loss of jobs, and alienating anyone who would help you! I have seen this many more times than the other more obvious issues as a reason for ongoing chaos in a person's life. They have no idea how they are contributing to the problems in their lives. Have you ever met someone who is overly self-important and expects everyone to cater to his or her needs? Have you ever met someone who is just plain mean and seems to have something nasty to say all the time? Have you ever met people who seem to act so helpless that it is a full-time job to be around them, because they always need something? Often people can get away with these offensive characteristics because someone is willing to put up with them. They may be able to stay in a job because they have extraordinary skill in an area or because it is really hard to find someone willing to do the job they have. However, there can be a shift in their universe: the job goes away; their skill becomes obsolete; the person they have been with dies or just decides they have had enough. Then what? Well, they don't think they have a problem. They have been like this for a long time, and for some reason it has worked so far. Not only do they think they don't have a problem, but they wouldn't have a clue how to do things differently even if they admitted they were the problem. Now invite someone with any one of these issues into your home and the "fun" begins.

I believe that everything I have, I have because God has blessed me with it. My house is really God's house. So when I felt God was asking me to make an extra bedroom available, it didn't seem an unreasonable request. But then it got deeper. I needed to allow this person to feel at home. It needed to be a safe place emotionally so she could recover from the difficult life circumstances that had brought her to this place of being without her own home. God began to challenge me on my need to correct things that were truly petty. I am sure you would not think them petty because I didn't. But it was obvious God thought them petty. They were things like which drawer kitchen utensils should go in or where to put the pots and pans. These are the things of everyday life. For my husband it was safety issues—unlocked doors and curling irons left on, etc. (all things I have done at some time or another, but I'm his wife, so he has to put up with me). When you live with someone, the little irritations become big things because you are faced with them every day. With a family member, you work things out or get used to certain things. But with a person you don't know, you have no systems for working things out. Ignoring things often leads to stuffing emotions that eventually erupt in overreactions. I saw these issues become the stuff of drama in the residential treatment programs I have supervised. Often the underlining issue was a sense of being disrespected. For people who are trying to find their dignity again, this can be a huge issue. With our guest, after I got a clue that I needed to just ignore some of the things that in the grand scheme were really unimportant, she then became less defensive, less demanding, and calmer. She began to heal. I really think that was why God brought her to us in the first place. It wasn't really about housing at all, but about healing.

I wasn't easy to live with because I was so guarded and often unfriendly. Trust is a huge factor when having someone in your home. She had some major barriers to getting a place, and it took her a long time. She always insisted she was plenty motivated not to have to live in someone else's home. She was used to having her own. But her options were so limited that we were never sure that we weren't the least of undesirable choices. That was a horrible way to live, being guarded and afraid to be too hospitable. The stress of that took its toll on Paul and me. We are glad we were able to help. We, and she, are glad she finally found a place. But when we help others, it almost always requires more than we are at first willing to give. But it almost always gives us back more than we ever expected to get.

I learned a lot more about myself and my own areas of selfishness that I needed to work on. I know my close friends thought I was a saint through it all, but I wasn't. God just kept reminding me of how blessed I am and of how much He has given me. I don't just mean in terms of material things, because none of that can be counted on. Material things may be in abundance today, but none of us know what tomorrow brings. I am thankful for the mercy I am given, I am talking about God's patience with my issues—the things I refuse to surrender,the things I keep doing over and over even after I know I need to stop. ! God helped me to see my house guest as his most beloved daughter, who was going through a hard enough time without my constantly reminding her that she was in someone else's home. When we move beyond our own selfish needs and desires, we mature in unexpected ways. I was constantly in a battle with my conscience about my own comfort and the needs of this person. One day the Lord showed me that when he talked about "the least of these my brethren," he was talking about whoever we define as the least of these. They aren't defined by education or wealth or social status, but by whoever we have an issue with. Who do we see as undeserving of our help and attention? Jesus told his disciples that however they treated the least of these was how they would be judged as having treated Jesus on the day of judgment (Matthew 25:45).

When God leads us to help someone, He knows them and us. Sometimes people act out of the goodness of their heart and not with any discernment or common sense. They invite someone in and get robbed or worse. They get mad at God for not protecting them. God will protect us when He leads us, but sometimes He will allow us to suffer for a greater purpose. There is a famous passage in the fictional book *Les Misérables*, by Victor Hugo. In the story a man is destitute, with no place to live and nothing to eat. A priest takes him into his home and feeds him and allows him to stay the night. In the middle of the night, the man robs the priest of all the silver he can find. The man is apprehended by the police and is brought to the priest's home, along with everything the man had stolen. The priest pretends that he had given the man the items as a gift and says (paraphrasing), "I am so glad you brought him back. Sir, you forgot the silver candlesticks." Most of us would not have been so gracious. But that act of kindness transforms this man. If we aren't up to being robbed and taken advantage of, we had better use some common sense in who we allow access to life and property. The truth is that we have very limited information about people until we live with them. It is almost always unwise to invite a stranger into your home. In the Christian community, we expect that someone who proclaims to be a believer will share the same value system. You cannot assume someone shares your values without having some history with him or her. An example is that pedophiles will never introduce themselves as such. If you have children or anyone who is particularly vulnerable like someone mentally disabled, physically handicapped, or a fragile senior citizen in your home, beware of taking in a stranger. A single man is usually less vulnerable than a single woman. Men are more often than women to be sexual predators, or to be violent, but women can be too.

Having cautioned you against taking in a stranger, let us talk about the exceptions. First, I advise you to pray and ask for guidance and protection. Take precautions until you know someone. Don't bed a stranger down in a room with your child. Don't give them keys to your house. Don't give them access to your checkbook, credit cards, and mail. Don't leave your female family members alone with a man you don't know well. Don't leave your male family member alone with a female stranger—not because you don't trust him, but because you might not be able to trust her. Some women will use the threat of an accusation, which would ruin his reputation or even possibly land him in jail, as leverage for blackmail. When it is possible, find out about them from others who know them and can vouch for them as safe people.

Be sure to coach your children on how to take precautions with someone staying with you. Do this even if it is a relative or friend. Most children are molested by someone known to the family. When you allow someone to stay in your home, you send a silent message to your children that this person is safe. Warn your boys as well as your girls. As a counselor and parenting instructor, I have met many men who have been molested as children. No matter how nice a person seems, you don't know if he or she has an addiction or even a mental problem.

Some individuals make their livelihood from suing people. They fall down in your driveway and sue for the homeowner's insurance money. I know it can be hard to still want to help if you face the realities of taking risks with people of questionable character. I have found some of the people who look the scariest to have the biggest hearts. I have seen people who have turned their lives around from addiction and criminal behavior to become pillars in their families and communities. I have a close friend who is one who came from a life of addictions to becoming a respected minister and leader. All people are worthy of our love and respect as human beings created in the image of God. God loves us, but even God gives us boundaries of acceptable behavior. An honest person will respect and appreciate your need for caution with someone new. Trust must be earned, only love is unconditional. If you do not have good personal boundaries, sharing a house with someone is probably not for you. If you need assistance in maturing in this area, I highly recommend the book *Boundaries* by Townsend and Cloud.

If you want to help those who are homeless, there are many ways to do so. Volunteer at a shelter or food bank. Serve on the board of a service organization. Donate to organizations that provide services. Donations can be cash or products that are needed, like hygiene products or blankets. You can make a bigger impact if you rally others and to donate and serve. Often groups will do a drive for hygiene products and then assemble kits to be given out. Many churches in the Los Angeles area do an Undie Sunday, which is a drive for new underwear to give to the shelters housing homeless individuals.

If you are faced with a friend or relative in need, consider first what you are able and willing to do. Then consider how it will impact your family. Will it jeopardize your own housing? Some apartment leases specify the number of people who can reside in the home. Is it even the best solution? Sometimes people don't want to deal with the consequences of their choices and expect family or friends to take up the slack. Is there a plan? If they stay with you this week, what then? Decide ahead of time the rules you want them to adhere to and give them in writing. Don't assume they will know what you expect. An example might be, "Don't bring others into my home without my permission." Decide if they can use your house phone. How late can people call? Can they come and go at all hours of the day and night? Can they smoke, drink, or use drugs in your house? If not, spell it out. If you give them a list in writing, it is not only clear but can be less accusatory. Decide what they will provide and what you will provide. Are they responsible for their own food, laundry detergent, and hygiene products? Are they expected to participate in household chores? Define what chores they are responsible to do and when. Decide how you will introduce them to people outside the home. Are they your house guest, a friend, a renter? You may be asked to give a reference for this person for housing or for a job. Decide whether you are willing or not.

I worked as a social worker for the county of San Bernardino for a couple of years in their in-home supportive services division. It was my job to help medically fragile individuals who needed assistance to remain in their homes. I was in charge of their caregivers in that

I had to determine if they were giving adequate care, and I had to approve their payment for services. The patient was my primary client; it was my job to make sure they were getting appropriate and adequate care. At least 50 percent of my clients were cared for by a family member. It became quite clear early in the job that I needed to be a counselor to these caregivers, who were often overwhelmed and ill equipped to meet all of the challenges they would face. I learned to help those who didn't want to be caregivers find other options for their loved ones. The ones who felt forced into giving care would ultimately suffer emotionally and sometimes cause undue suffering to the one they were trying to help. Not everyone is able to handle caring for a loved one in the home. In such cases, I would encourage them to hire a caregiver and at the very least make sure they weren't taking on the responsibility 24/7. I took my own advice when my eighty-five-year-old mother came to live with me. At first her care was minimal, but as her needs grew, I needed more help. The best thing I could do for my mother was to get help so I wouldn't become overwhelmed or sick myself. In the end her needs were so great that I was not sure that I wouldn't have to hospitalize her. I ended up utilizing hospice care, which was a great help. Even with a caregiver and hospice nurses, the stress of my mother's decline was so taxing that I became ill as a result of the stress. My mother was easy to care for, in contrast to some of the clients I had as a social worker. I had a good relationship with my mother. She was a kind and good person. Even so it was difficult. Though I had other options, it was my desire to allow her to be in a familiar and comfortable place where she was surrounded by those who loved her. Hard as it was, it was my great privilege to allow her to die at home, which she did, peacefully, in her own room with her family. Some of you may be confronted with caring for someone who is not your family, or a family member who is very difficult. It isn't always a good idea to say yes to this challenge. I have known people who have said yes to caring for a family member, and it has resulted in their driving away their own spouse. Please be realistic about what you and your family are able to do. If you feel this is something God would have you do, He will give you the strength and show you the way. However, sometimes we mistake guilt, or a sense of duty, as the voice of God. Be sure you know the difference. Of course, sometimes family needs us and we have no other realistic option. Sometimes we take on a task we know is too difficult for us, because we feel there aren't any other viable options. If this is you, remember we aren't meant to be alone in our distress. Ask for, seek out, and accept help.

CHAPTER 4

Definitions and Service Challenges:
Of the Temporarily Displaced and
the Chronically Homeless

Who Are the Homeless?

There are generally two primary categories of homeless individuals: individuals or families who are temporarily displaced due to economic or social circumstances, and those who have adopted life on the street as a lifestyle. The second group is commonly referred to as chronically homeless. This group is more resistant to interventions. The first group can move into the second category if no timely intervention occurs.

Recently Displaced Profiles

In America, these individuals include those fleeing domestic abuse, dependent adults kicked out of their family's home, families evicted, those leaving shelters for inappropriate behavior or because their time was up, those released from jail or prison, the mentally ill who have wandered away from home or care facilities, and those displaced by natural disasters. Most emotionally and socially healthy individuals do not end up on the street because they have a network of family and friends who would take them in and help them get back on their feet. The problem comes when the normal network of support is interrupted or the displaced person has such poor life skills that he or she has either alienated those who would have helped them and/or does not have the ability to access other resources. Sometimes those who function well in society and who have a strong network of support are overcome by catastrophic circumstances, like those made homeless by a major natural disaster. In a natural disaster or in war an entire community can be destroyed. This can cause people to lose their entire network of support. Sometimes it is catastrophic events in an individual's life that derail their ability to cope. The impact of a traumatic crisis can make it difficult to do normal tasks, like filling out an application or going to a government office to talk to someone about getting help. People who are so traumatized that they can't reach out for help can become homeless very quickly. Most Americans live paycheck to paycheck with little if any reserve. The single person who goes into a coma and is hospitalized for a long period of time can wake up to having been evicted, all their possessions thrown away, and a huge hospital bill. Ask yourself, "Who would take care of my personal and professional business if I was temporarily incapacitated?"

Sometimes adults who might have been able to live on their own have not been properly prepared or incentivized to develop those life skills. Let us define a *dependent adult* as one who has become or remained dependent on others for his or her financial support. These individuals include those who are dependent on their spouse or significant other for all financial support, adult children who continue to be supported by their parents or others, and those who must depend on others due to physical or mental disabilities. We will take a closer look at the homeless mentally ill in the next chapter. When dependent adults become homeless and have no resources other than the street or charitable organizations, it is usually because they lack life skills to acquire and maintain a job, and they have not learned to manage their financial responsibilities. Their only skills may be some behaviors they use to get others to care for their needs. They may not know how or even desire to acquire the new skills needed to be independent. This often occurs after the death of the one who has taken care of them. Now they are dealing with the loss of the one who brought safety and order to their life and the necessity of caring for themselves.

Dependent adults also include those who are impaired by an addiction, which makes it impossible for them to function sufficiently to support themselves. Displaced individuals often have so alienated their providers that they are kicked out (sometimes being driven to a rescue mission or treatment facility and left), or they flee because the situation with their provider becomes intolerable.

Most of these individuals are resistant to sociological and spiritual interventions that would produce long-term success because they generally see their problem as one of geography rather than poor life skills. The displaced mentally ill are often the most difficult to assist because they require medically trained staff to stabilize their medications and administer appropriate treatment. They are also often resistant to the care that would help them. Even if they receive appropriate treatment, they often leave treatment once they are stable, believing they no longer need help because they are better. It is only when they become sufficiently unstable that they either become willing to get assistance or are arrested or deemed a danger to themselves or others by law enforcement. Homelessness is not considered by law enforcement or the courts as being a danger to self. This is very sad, for the mentally ill can be fully delusional, and so long as they aren't physically assaulting themselves or others, they are left to wander the streets dirty and malnourished until they commit a crime or become the victim of a crime. They may be raped, beaten, and robbed. In their delusional state, they make a poor witness to any crime. Their condition, for example, paranoia, may make them incapable of seeking effective help. If they are treated roughly by law enforcement, they may identify all police as the enemy and will not seek help. When there is funding for it, social services departments have created teams to go to the homeless and try to get them to the needed services. Whether it is a social services team or rescue mission staff, trust will be an essential element that must be established before help will be embraced.

Chronically Homeless or Homelessness as a Lifestyle

These individuals have crossed from looking for a way to rejoining conventional society to trying to *make their life work within the context of homelessness.* They often have had so many failures at remaining financially and socially stable that it seems easier to adjust to living in shelters or on the streets. Usually they have been displaced for a while and out of necessity had to learn survival skills. They develop a system that works for them, and they begin to take pride in their independence and survival skills.

Each day has its own set of challenges, but they are simple and straightforward. They find a place to sleep, sources of food, and drug connections if applicable and panhandle or develop small street businesses for cash. They develop relationships that will serve as companionship, safety, and information on resources. It can be a very harsh world. They may be assaulted, robbed, and raped. They may become indebted to loan sharks or others who prey on their vulnerability and become involved in drug trafficking, prostitution, robberies, and con games.

They learn the resources in the area, including rescue missions and how to work the various systems to their best advantage. Some travel from city to city using the shelter systems until they are no longer eligible. Then they move on to another city and do the same thing until enough time has passed to begin the circuit again. They learn how to tell the institutions like the rescue missions what they want to hear to make them eligible for a bed and other resources. They become acquainted with the social services programs and learn the correct responses to get on the payroll for General Relief or for Social Security Insurance. As a counselor in a shelter setting, I learned to recognize the clients who have become institutionalized. Institutionalization means that they only know how to function within the framework of an institutional setting. They often self-sabotage when it comes time to graduate from a program. They just don't know how to do life on the outside. This is especially true of those who have been incarcerated for most of their lives. The freedom of choice involved in living a life outside of the regimented prison life is overwhelming. When people are in an institution, like prison, so many of their daily decisions are made for them that the multitude of choices and decisions necessary in an unstructured life can be overwhelming. I have heard the difference in a day can be between three thousand and thirty-five thousand decisions.

As an example of the sophistication that can evolve in a homeless lifestyle, I'd like to share an extreme case. When I worked for Battered Women's Services in San Diego, I found that, among chronically homeless women, it was believed that the battered women's shelters were often nicer than the regular homeless shelters. They tend to be cleaner, with more space per person and fewer rules, and the food was better. It was also possible to stay inside all day, in contrast to many shelters that put their people out after breakfast, and they can't come back until the evening. Some homeless women would make up stories about abuse to get into the nicer shelter. We, as shelter counselors and hotline workers, had to develop methods of screening out these imposters. We weren't always successful, wanting to err on the side of believing people rather than denying shelter to someone who really needed it. One such client was a woman who had four children with her. She also claimed to be blind. After we admitted her to the shelter, several factors made her story suspicious, but the incident that really brought it to light was when she forgot she was supposed to be blind and read something off a bulletin board behind me. We transitioned her to the homeless shelter. Three years later, I was working as a supervisor in the shelter and overheard a hotline worker talking to a blind woman with four children. All the names had changed, but the ages of the children matched, and the story was almost identical. She had just been going to other shelters around the country, expecting that by the time she got back to San Diego, California, there wouldn't still be anyone working there who remembered her. There is a high turnover of service staff, so this was a pretty good plan. As long as the names were different, nothing in the computer would trigger her as a problem client.

One of the problems we had in helping the women in the domestic violence shelter get help was that if we sent them to the welfare office without a staff escort, there were predatory men who would approach them. Some of these men would look for a woman with several children, knowing her checks would be larger. They would be friendly, helpful, and interested in everything about her. The naïve women who allowed these men into their lives found out eventually that they were really only interested in her checks. Sometimes they were also sexual predators who wanted to abuse her children. We also frequently had people offer very low-rent or even free rooms for the women. The problem was that some of these people were predators looking for women to exploit. We had many women who came to us after trying to enter the United States illegally, only to be exploited by the men who promised them a new life. They were raped, robbed, and enslaved. One such woman had been raped and left to die at the side of the road. A homeless man found her and gave her his boxer shorts and his shirt to cover herself and helped her get to a hospital. The hospital social worker contacted us. It is unlikely they even examined her, as we had to send her back for treatment after she realized the boxer shorts were full of crabs (lice). This poor woman had been beaten and raped and then had to deal with this horrible infestation in her pubic region. I was the only counselor on duty who spoke any Spanish, and she had to try and communicate the problem to me, a stranger who barely spoke her language.

Many people who come from other countries trying to escape the woes of their own country only find that they are selling themselves into slavery here. Many of the immigrant men I met going through the recovery programs came to the United States hoping for a better life. When they couldn't find work or housing, they became depressed and turned to alcohol and/or drugs. They were so beaten down by addiction that they became a shell of their former selves. Some of my own family members couldn't understand why I would want to work with this population. When all you can see is the despair, the dirt, and the hopelessness, it is understandable to want to turn away. But when you see despair become hope, and the grime is washed away to reveal a person who has self-respect again, it is a very different experience. I couldn't help but be moved when I saw these lives revived by the power of a little love and compassion. The human spirit can overcome great obstacles when we know we have worth. Depression and despair can rob us our humanity. I believe there is no greater truth than the knowledge that we are loved by God and that He has a plan and purpose for our lives if we will embrace it. What if you could be part of the restoration of hundreds of lives? What if you could see God restore hope, faith, health, and yes even wealth? I have seen families that have shed the heritage of abuse and have become the inspiration for other families to step out of destructive life patterns. I stood in the chapel of a mission one day and watched as about two hundred residents of the program poured their hearts out to God in worship. It was so beautiful, so genuine. I thought of Jesus's words to his host when they were interrupted by a woman who was on the bottom of the social ladder:

"A certain creditor had two debtors; one owed five hundred denarii, and the other fifty. When they could not pay, he forgave them both. Now which of them will love him more?" Simon answered, "The one, I suppose, to whom he forgave more." And he said to him, "You have judged rightly." Then turning toward the woman he said to Simon, "Do you see this woman? I entered your house, you gave me no water for my feet, but she has wet my feet with her tears and wiped them with her hair. You gave me no kiss, but from the time I came in she has not ceased to kiss my feet. You did not anoint my head with oil, but she has anointed my feet with ointment. Therefore I tell you, her sins, which are many, are forgiven, for she loved much; but he who is forgiven little, loves little." (Luke 7:42–47)

Working with those who recognize that they have been "forgiven much" has truly spoiled me for working with America's average congregation. The level of gratitude to God for a new life and a new start is a joy to witness. The truth is that all of us are in need of forgiveness and acceptance; some of us are just more aware than others.

CHAPTER 5

Interventions to Homelessness

Interventions for the homeless service worker can be broken down into *first contact, intake, initial stabilization, short-term rehabilitation, long-term rehabilitation,* and *aftercare.*

First Contact—Who, What, and When

Who makes the first contact?

Most homeless individuals find their way to resources through personal referral from people they meet on the street, from outreach teams, social services, the courts, jails, and police. A few are referred by family, friends, or churches. A few have enough skill or divine providence to find them on their own.

What are they looking for?

They usually come looking for the necessities of life: food, bathroom facilities, clothing, medical assistance, and shelter. If they are recently displaced, they are usually looking for *the fast track to reinstatement of what was familiar and comfortable.* If they have been on the streets for a while or repeatedly, they may be looking *for a break, a place to rest up, or they may be ready for real change.* When change is the goal, they usually say they are tired of living the way they have been and realize they need assistance to make a change. Sometimes they have been raped, shot, robbed, or beaten. *In a state of crisis, they are looking for compassion, comfort, and safety. It is during these times of crisis that they are most likely to seek real help to get off the street.*

The first contact usually involves meeting the need of one or more of the essentials of life: human kindness, food, personal hygiene facilities, clothing, shelter, and medical care. These are the door openers to assisting a homeless person. If first contact doesn't meet a basic need, it is unlikely to be successful.

When does a first contact lead to further help?

When a first contact inspires hope that something better than their current situation is available to them at a cost that seems reasonable to them, a homeless person might take the next step. I'm not talking about a monetary cost but an emotional and energy cost. These are individuals at the end of their emotional and physical tethers.

Intake

Intake is the verbal and written process necessary to describe their need and access resources. Poor communication due to mental illness, drug impairment, and acute emotional distress can be impediments for a homeless person negotiating this process. All resource entities (individuals, churches, service organizations, social services) have criteria that must be met by the applicant.

Government assistance almost always requires legal identity documents in order to access services. Not having a recognized identification card or birth certificate or social security card can mean the difference between continued independence or homelessness. Only shelters and churches generally provide any extended assistance without these documents.

Service organizations, whether they are secular nonprofits or faith-based organizations, focus on the applicant promising to comply with rules set forth for their clients. They usually include things like showing up on time for appointments and non–abusive speech and behavior.

The intake process itself can be traumatic or empowering. The fear of being shamed or rejected produces less-than-reliable information in the initial data-gathering process. Applicants will withhold valuable information about themselves and their challenges. They often give less-than-truthful information about drug use, citizenship, marital status, child custody issues, mental illness, medical condition, criminal history, and probation status. The intake process must be viewed as a first step, not an end in itself.

Initial Stabilization—Emotional and Physical

Emotional Care

Unconditional positive regard, food, hygiene, medical help, shelter, and sleep are the first concerns in the stabilization of a homeless person. Kindness and authentic love are the most important ingredients. People will choose to sleep in dirty clothes or go hungry with a person who makes them feel valued, rather than live in a pristine shelter where they are treated as though they are subhuman. That having been said, the appearance and cleanliness of the environment in which we house homeless individuals speaks volumes about how much we value and care about them. At this stage the person is almost always in a crisis of some form. Emotional support and validation are crucial. Simple things like being smiled at, having eye contact, being recognized by name, and having small needs addressed become crucial to creating a safe emotional environment. Their physical environment needs to communicate safety and comfort. There should not be too much drama, loud sounds, or threats like disease, insects, vermin, or cold or heat. I have been in a shelter setting where many of these negative environmental conditions were present within the building, but because the staff slept in the environment with them, some of the negative impact was mitigated. The message from the greater society was still one of shame and devaluing them.

Physical Restoration

Homeless people are often recovering from abuse to their bodies from any number of sources. Drug abuse and the need to detoxify are very common, but also to recover from being exposed to the elements, poor nutrition, physical abuse, and sleep deprivation.

The homeless individual is almost always physically and emotionally exhausted. They come in from a survival mode in which they were running on adrenalin, and when they let down, they may crash for two to three days before they can function even at a minimal level. That means that they only hear a fraction of what is said to them, including rules, requirements, and instructions. Activities and requirements need to be kept to a minimum, and positive, supportive attention needs to be available whenever they are ready to receive it. Simple voluntary group activities are sometimes helpful in bridging the way back into social communication and a sense of belonging. Whether in someone's home or in a shelter setting, allowing the person to do something that will benefit someone else often helps them feel less helpless. An example of the helped becoming the helper is seen in battered women's shelters that have been started by women who had left an abusive relationship and were now reaching out to other women in a similar position. Individuals in shelter settings usually are happy to assist in activities that further the helping organization. The opportunity to give back helps them envision themselves as people with something to offer, not just needy recipients.

CHAPTER 6

Short-Term Rehabilitation

For the sake of discussion, let us define short-term re-habilitation as a period of intervention with a homeless individual of not less than three months and not more than one year. The goal of homeless individuals is usually to achieve a level of financial and residential indepen-dence; in other words, a place of their own, and a means to support an independent lifestyle. The goal of most re-source entities is the same as the client, except that their concepts of what will accomplish that goal over the long term are often different from that of the client. At this stage clients are beginning to evaluate their choices and options. They need information that will enlarge their view of the chain of events that led to their current situ-ation. Most people can bounce back from setbacks. If the person is recently displaced and has had a relatively stable lifestyle, some short-term help may be all they need.

It usually takes a series of events or failures to produce homelessness. One could blame homelessness on drug or alcohol addiction, but there are many more addicts who are not homeless than ones who are. None of the factors we see in homelessness are by themselves predictors of long-term homelessness. This is not true in all countries, but in America it is more difficult to become homeless. In short-term rehabilitation, there is less time to devote to the deeper issues that may cause the person to spiral down again. The focus by the very nature of the time element must be focused on stabilizing the person physically and emotionally and helping them acquire resources that will lead to independence as quickly as possible.

A case management plan, which can be as informal as a list of goals, needs to be established. Clients must define what they believe success will look like. They will not be motivated to achieve anything else. This initial plan should be revealed at least in part in the intake process to determine if the resource entity and the client are a compatible match. The resource entity will have its own idea of what success will look like to them. Then a structure of activities and behavioral goals needs to be identified, which will produce incremental progress toward the goals. There are some easily identifiable obstacles to self-sufficiency.

Obstacles to producing an income, like lack of education, training, or experience, can be addressed. Poor health, hygiene, or behavioral habits can be explored. A personal history that limits opportunities, like being undocumented or a criminal history, can be evaluated, and a strategy for most effectively dealing with it needs to be devised. Sometimes it becomes clear that additional help will be needed because solving the problems will take longer than a short-term process allows. Then part of the short-term plan is getting the person into a longer-term process. On the short term, the person might complete a GED program, but the long-term goal might be to prepare him or her after to enter a community college program. A short-term goal could be to discover what the person's health problems are and how he or she will determine what jobs he or she can do. Serious long-term health concerns may necessitate an application for long-term disability insurance. A client could begin the process and enroll in vocational training that is designed for someone with his or her particular limitations.

More often the real underlying problem that is destabilizing the individual is the inability to make good choices with regard to relationships. They either choose untrustworthy and destructive partners or are themselves untrustworthy and destructive. Often it is both themselves and the people they choose who are dysfunctional.

Anger management, domestic violence, parenting, and twelve-step groups are helpful with these social and behavioral problems. The group setting allows for feedback that can be helpful in recognizing faulty thinking and behavior. Other living and working environments that provide healthy feedback will assist the homeless person in having an enlarged view of what is possible. If all you have been exposed to is dysfunctional behavior, you will not even be able to imagine another course of action. Seeing people around them make different choices and get different results begins to plant the possibility of living life better.

Generally, homeless individuals suffer from a combination of problems that have to do with both financial and social problems. Even the victims of a natural disaster like Katrina may have been very stable prior to the event, but the compounded loss of loved ones, friends, their community, and property left many people so traumatized that it was not practical to expect them to acquire new jobs, new communities, and new friends and go on as if nothing had happened. A period of depression and grieving is very normal but can be very debilitating. At least in a natural disaster, you are not alone in the tragedy. There are many sympathetic ears, and people are generally supportive. But what of the people whose spouses divorces them. They care for a sick child until they have to give up their job, and then the child dies. If we approach these individuals who have faced a long series of traumas as though they just need a job and housing, we will destine them to recycle through the same process over and over. Hope and genuine care, coupled with time, are the elements of healing needed when tragedy is compounded.

A Story of Grief and Healing

I once knew a woman who was the antithesis of someone you would expect to be homeless. She had come from a reasonably stable childhood. She had what was regarded by most people as a good relationship with her husband. They were both avid church attenders, he had a great job that paid for a beautiful house in a nice area of town, and they drove new cars. She didn't work outside the home but busied herself with volunteer work and being the perfect wife for her successful husband. It seemed to work for them for many years until her husband became depressed and addicted to prescription pain killers. His addiction spiraled out of control, and he ended up on the streets using illegal drugs. They lost everything. She started using drugs as well and even followed him into homelessness. She eventually got counseling and left him. He committed suicide after she left him. She came to a rescue mission because she was homeless and addicted. Her chaplain realized she would not be successful in helping this woman unless she addressed the grief and guilt that were keeping her in a destructive cycle. They ended up going to a grief support group together. Working through the grief and her issues of codependency were more important than any job training or housing assistance she received. Finally, someone was able to see past her geography to the pain in her soul, which gave her the support she needed to heal.

Spiritual Care

I believe it is within the transforming power of God that ultimate healing comes. However, this spiritual transformation is not a topical salve we can lather on. It is the spiritual dimension that made the twelve step groups powerful, and those who have minimized Christ in these groups have denied the power that transformed so many lives. Jesus didn't ram the gospel down anyone's throat but instead said, "Come and see" and "Follow me." Study of the Bible and the introduction to the Spirit of God through Jesus Christ will assist a person in beginning to have a map charting the new life. The great thing about this spiritual birth is that is isn't dependent on any one person for its continuance. Getting a person interested in having this experience is accomplished with the "Jesus method": "Come and see" and "follow me." It was on the way, and in the process of everyday life, that Jesus's disciples "got it." It is this inner transformation that will have the most lasting impact. That inner transformation is embraced when it is seen lived out before them in the lives of those offering help. The love of God is the most important ingredient in any recovery, short or long term. Even in short-term care, we can trust that Christ will complete the good work, which he began in us. I am paraphrasing here a promise made by the apostle Paul to the Philippian Christians who were struggling with some of the same issues of being social outcasts (Phil. 1.6).

CHAPTER 7

Long-Term Rehabilitation

Long-term rehabilitation, for the sake of discussion, shall be defined as not less than one year. Jesus took three years to create twelve disciples, and one of them didn't make it. Eleven of these disciples, though they stumbled and fell at the end of the three years, were able to rise up again, remain strong, and change the world around them. In looking at recidivism rates, we do well to remember even Jesus had one who turned back. All of the disciples had doubts when they were first left on their own. It took the resurrection and power of the Holy Spirit to put them back on track. The first six months are basically recovery from physical and emotional trauma. Once people begin to feel normal, — non-traumatized—they begin to crave a normal routine. They want to get back to work, or to their family or to go shopping for a mate. It is only when they recognize that *business as usual has never really worked for very long* that they become willing to remain in a new environment long enough to explore the deeper issues.

The need to stop grieving and have fun and do things that break the tension experienced over the first six months becomes very pressing. A balance between challenges to old ways of thinking and opportunities to experience success needs to be established. Activity needs to increase, and the need to see progress becomes paramount. These deeper issues are quite painful and begin to emerge just as the individual thinks he or she is done with trauma and grieving. Without appropriate support, these deeper issues will be pressed down, and a need to appear normal becomes paramount. *The person who becomes incredibly happy and overly competent is often at greatest risk for relapse.* There must be an atmosphere that allows for the admission that there is still much to do, while we rejoice in the victories already achieved. This is where the level of training and experience in the staff of a supportive service becomes crucial. The helping professionals must at this point be able to inspire hope and discern the true areas of need. Relationships of accountability and support are also crucial to this stage. In a church setting, mature Christians with spiritual discernment need to be willing to invest time and attention for their spiritual siblings to continue to grow and mature. Tasks that test character, consistency, and follow-through will expose the areas of need and give opportunity for further growth. It is essential that there remain room for accepting faltering steps, so that no fear of mistakes steals the real prize. Teachers must be willing to give their pupils opportunities to succeed and to fail. Christ must increase, and we must decrease. Jesus did not see himself as a failure because Peter would falter in following him. He knew Peter had to go through the process of failure as part of learning about the need for strength from God rather than his own determination. He saw that failure as part of Peter's personal learning curve and told Peter "when once you have turned again, strengthen your brothers" (NASB, Luke 22.32). Service organizations that create incredible programs and op-portunities for homeless individuals sometimes become too focused on a marketable product at the end. Clients sometimes feel like they have to pretend they are more healed than they really are. We must not forget that learning is a lifelong process. In 1 Corinthians 3:7 the great church planter, the apostle Paul tells us that some plant, others water, but it is God who gives the increase.

CHAPTER 8

Aftercare

The Close of a Relationship

We cannot befriend, mentor, and even parent these individuals through the journey of discovery, healing, and
change and then just drop them like a worn-out shoe.
The process does not end at a point on a calendar. Just
as successful parenting helps to bridge a child's transition

from the home into the world by introducing them to others who will teach them and care for them and help them grow. Though the nature of the relationship changes, hopefully a new dimension allows for continued affection and respect. We can do no less with those with whom we have walked through what is perhaps the most difficult time in their lives. The parent must push the child out of the nest to fly on his or her own but must also continue to be the child's greatest cheer leader. There is a great sense of loss and abandonment that occurs when clients are cut off from those who have had such an important impact on their lives. No one will appreciate their successes to the same degree as those who have seen the struggle. Few will continue to believe in them if they stumble for a moment as they walk on their own. It should not be a relationship that breeds dependence but one that offers moral support, encouragement, and a cheering section. If this is done successfully, the client will emerge with a sense of confidence and independence and still be able to value the relationships that helped make that possible. If it is not done appropriately, clients will sometimes sabotage their own progress in an attempt to remain in the dependent relationship.

Countering Institutionalization

Some clients become institutionalized, meaning they can function well within a residential program but can't function successfully outside a program environment. If the end of a program means they are alone and vulnerable again, they may feel as though they have accomplished nothing. If they have not reestablished (or perhaps established for the first time) their confidence in who they are and what they can accomplish, the world may overwhelm them.

Many individuals who become homeless come out of the foster care system. When children hit eighteen it is said they age out of the system. Though a few children are placed with loving families who treat them as their own children, most do not enjoy such stability. They are often shifted from family to family and back and forth to their birth parents or a group home. When they leave one foster family, they usually never hear from them again. Think about how you would see the world if as a child your parents died and you were taken from your home and from your siblings and put in the home of strangers. Now you are very angry and sad and aren't the easiest child to deal with. So you live with another family for two years, and they decide you are just too much to handle and give you back to children's services.

This can happen two to five or more times in the child's life. Now these people are adults and haven't been able to stay financially stable. They have no family to go to and ask for help. They enter a program depressed and with their life in chaos. Loving counselors shower them with encouragement and tell them God loves them. Then it comes time to leave the program. For these adults, it can be a replay of their experience leaving foster care. They can feel abandoned and lost, despite having done well in the program.

We all need to see ourselves in the way God sees us. God sees us as "overcomers," as "beloved children," as "ambassadors of Christ." He will never leave us or forsake us. When clients have had the world reflect an image of themselves as being of less value than the rest of the human race, as a person unworthy of being seen, heard, or helped, it can take some time to change their mental picture of themselves. Over the years, many clients have told me that after they left the residential treatment program, they could still hear my voice in their head, encouraging or correcting them in the tasks of life. Most of us carry the sound of our parents' words in our heads, but what if those words were never words of encouragement but only words of shame?

Celebrating Progress

Aftercare is just what the name implies. Someone still cares after the main victories are celebrated. These occasions for celebrating their continued progress are important in keeping a sense of connectedness to those who see their progress and achievements.

One of the things long-term members of twelve-step programs often refer to are celebrations and tokens given for anniversaries of sobriety. Little mementos like lapel pins, or a cake at a group meeting, are spoken of as though they were made of gold. It is important to teach those who have overcome great difficulties to celebrate their successes. The celebration of getting a place of their own can help them to dwell on the progress forward instead of what they have lost. The person who lost a big house, multiple cars, and the right to live with their own children may find it difficult to celebrate getting a small studio apartment. However, with the help of those who care about them and their progress, they can see it for what it is: a step in the right direction, as opposed to continuing to spiral downward.

The other consideration that becomes very important for the person who has received help is to give back in some way. They may become a sponsor or a volunteer or give financially. It is a way of redeeming those awful things by turning them into an opportunity to help someone else. There are two kinds of relapse. One is that which occurs without support, in secret. That is the kind that Judas had. He betrayed Christ, but he destroyed his own life instead of reaching out for forgiveness and help. Peter denied Christ, but the door of relationship remained open between him and Jesus and between Peter and the other disciples. Jesus's advice to him was to help others once he recovered from stumbling. In Proverbs 24:16 it says, "For a righteous man falls seven times, and rises again, But the wicked stumble in time of calamity" (NASB). If we have succeeded in establishing a connection between the client and Christ, and also with the body of believers, we have a much greater chance that they will rise like Peter. Aftercare is lifelong. That is why it is essential to connect them to a family that will live on long after an organization folded up shop or an individual has died. The body of Christ, the church universal, is that family. It is this very lack of connectedness that often leads to homelessness. They have no safety net when tragedy strikes.

CHAPTER 9

The Stigma of Homelessness

In conclusion, homelessness is a description of a physical circumstance, not the definition of a person's character or status. There is such a stigma with the label of homeless that it in itself becomes a trauma from which recovery is necessary. I am so glad Jesus once identified himself with the homeless when he said in Matthew 8:20, "And Jesus saith unto him, *the foxes have holes, and the birds of the air have nests; but the Son of man hath not where to lay his head"* (*21*[st] *Century KJV).*

May God help us to lay aside judgment and be his ambassadors in ministering to those in need. Let us serve those he brings across our path as though it is Christ himself to whom we minister.

> "Then the King will say to those on His
> right, 'Come, you who are blessed of My

Father, inherit the kingdom prepared for you from the foundation of the world. 35 For I was hungry, and you gave Me something to eat; I was thirsty, and you gave Me something to drink; I was a stranger, and you invited Me in; 36 naked, and you clothed Me; I was sick, and you visited Me; I was in prison, and you came to Me.' 37 Then the righteous will answer Him, 'Lord, when did we see You hungry, and feed You, or thirsty, and give You something to drink? 38 And when did we see You a stranger, and invite You in, or naked, and clothe You? 39 When did we see You sick, or in prison, and come to You?' 40 The King will answer and say to them, 'Truly I say to you, to the extent that you did it to one of these brothers of Mine, even the least of them, you did it to Me' (NASB, Matt. 24.34–40).

About the Author

Tina Babcock has a broad background working with impoverished, homeless, and addicted individuals and families. After working for several years in San Diego, California, with families impacted by domestic violence, she moved to the Los Angeles area and became a chaplain and administrator for a rescue mission in the heart of LA's Skid Row. Los Angeles has the largest homeless population in the United States. After three years as Executive director of the Anne Douglas Center, in charge of women and family programs for the Los Angeles Mission, she was recruited to help missions in several cities develop programs that went beyond feeding and housing homeless individuals. Chaplain Babcock became a regional director for City Mission Network over the Skid Row ministries of five other American cities: Chicago, Illinois, Colorado Springs, Colorado, Las Vegas, Nevada, and San Francisco and Chico, California. She traveled throughout the United States to shelters working with staff as a consultant and trainer and had the opportunity to examine the services offered in many American cities. She took a break from the mission work to complete work on a book and spent two years working with medically fragile Medi-Cal recipients with Aging and Adult Services, San Bernardino County, as a social worker. She was recruited back to work at the mission in LA again, this time spending more time writing curriculum and mentoring staff. For the next eight years she would also serve as chaplain for the Los Angeles Police Department, Central Division, in the heart of Skid Row.

A convert to Christianity at the age of fourteen, her first community of faith was a house ministry that included teens and young adults coming out of drugs, prostitution, and criminal gangs. Leading her first Bible studies at the tender age of sixteen in a Christian club in her public high school, she has been a student of and teacher of biblical principles for more than four decades. She holds a bachelor's degree in psychology from Azusa Pacific University, Master's Level Addiction Specialist and Clinical Supervisor Certificates from The Breining Institute, and is a Certified Addiction Treatment Counselor. She served as a senior chaplain and administrator with the Los Angeles Mission for ten years, an LAPD chaplain for eight years, and an associate pastor in several protestant churches over the past thirty years. She now holds her current license and ordination under the ministry of which she also serves as CEO: Restoration and Recovery Resources Group, a nonprofit ministry specializing in equipping Christians in recovery ministries. She is part of the ministry team as an associate pastor at Christ Centered Community Church, in Chino, California. She is also an adjunct professor for Next Dimension University, a Christian Bible college, where she received a doctorate in religious studies. Tina Babcock is also a wife of more than forty years and mother of two daughters. She has been counseling individuals, couples, and families for almost twenty years. She is a prolific curriculum writer and an inspirational speaker. She is a passionate and inspiring keynote speaker, always engaging the audience and leaving them excited to put into practice in their own lives what has been shared. Having come from a childhood in which abuse threatened to define her life, she speaks from a place of healing and hope that inspires others to expect God's best in their lives. Her path to healing has opened opportunities to reach hundreds, perhaps thousands of lives in need of hope and restoration. Her favorite scripture is a good way to close this book:

> The Spirit of the Lord God is upon me;
> Because the Lord has anointed me to

preach the good news to the afflicted; He has sent me to bind up the broken hearted, to proclaim liberty to the captives and freedom to prisoners (NASB, Isaiah 61:1).

Bibliography

Kofman, Olga Loraine. *Deinstitutionalization and Its Discontents: American Mental Health Policy Reform.* CMC Senior Thesis. Claremont Colleges. Claremont: Scholarship@Claremont, 2012. <http://scholarship.claremont.edu/cmc_theses/342>.

Kuhnhenn, Jim. ""VA review finds 'significant and chronic' failures". bigstory.ap.org." Television News Journalist. June 27, 2014. Internet Video. 3 August 2016. <https://en.wikipedia.org/wiki/Veterans_Health_Administration_scandal_of_2014>.

Meghan Henry, Dr. Alvaro Cortes, Azim Shivji, and Katherine Buck, Abt Associates. *The 2014 Annual Homeless Assessment Report (AHAR)to Congress.* The U.S. Department of Community Planning and Development, 2014. website.

"Skid Row – Origens." Wickepedia article. 2016. website.

Thoma, Rick. "A Critical Look At The Foster Care System:." Web document. 2010. website.

Townsend, Henry Cloud and John. *Boundaries: When to say yes, when to say no to take control of your life.* Grand Rapids, Michigan: Zondervan Publishing House, 1992.

Made in the USA
Las Vegas, NV
01 September 2021

29372011R00069